Cotton Wool

by

Kineta Blackman

ISBN: 978-976-96903-0-1

Editing / Book Layout by

Passionate Words
Editing Services

(IG @passionate.words.editing246)

Dedication

This book is dedicated to the teenager or young adult who grew up with a Christian background and often doesn't fit in. You might feel like you're the only one who lives this way but this book is by a fellow misfit. You are not alone.

Acknowledgments

First of all, I want to thank God for the experiences which inspired me to write.

Next, I want to thank Robert Gibson and the entire Passionate Words Editing Services team for this opportunity to share my work with the world.

I also want to thank my family who is rooting for me and want the best for me.

Lastly, I would like to thank my friends who still hang around even with my poor friendship skills.

Table of Contents

Rain

Rain, fall. Tears.
Days ... weeks ... years.
Problems: trials, fears.
Rain, fall, tears.

Future, present, past –
Nothing that will last.
Future? Present. Past!
It all moves too fast.

You ask yourself, “Who cares?”

Rain? Fall. Tears.
Rain? Fall,
Rain ...

I smile.

Growth

Swinging wild in the dark,
Picked the target and missed the mark.
Missed it wide.
Woke up to find I've been left behind;
Missed the migration.
They probably tried to wake me,
But I didn't listen.

Blindfolded and spun around and around;
Disoriented, falling to the ground,
Helpless.
Reminded of a stupid decision in the past.
That dumb feeling you get when
You pour the juice and miss the glass.
Or walk into a transparent pane.
Should've seen it coming.

Only taking two when entitled four.

Could do with three.

What are you trying to prove?

No point worthy of mention

This downward spiral of folly

The consequences due to lack of careful thought

Washed down time's drain

With maturity's cleansing attribute –

Growth.

It happens.

Though not always seen.

Group Project

Everybody rushing,
Trying to get everywhere
In no time.
But this is a different kind of race.

Nobody waiting,
Getting nowhere
And making good time.
What a waste.

Each one helping,
Now we're getting somewhere!
But so little time.
Make haste!

Fuzz, Bubble & Pop!

Fuzz, bubble & pop!
Think warm and fuzzy-
like when I see you seeing me
and I can't stop smiling–
And I'm twiddling
My toes...
I'm glad that you're here-
but not how fast time goes!
And I'm doing cartwheels in my head
'til I'm dizzy and I have to stop.
See how you make me feel?
Like fuzz, bubble & pop!

Sand for Seashells

Glistening golden in the sun,
that heat under my feet
turning quick steps into run.
It's hard to get rid of;
I'm forever dusting foot and hand.
Yes. Exactly what I fear –
It's even in my hair!
But, I understand...
There must be sand for seashells.

Nothing to Offer

I bring

Nothing to stimulate conversation ... you leave me

Speechless.

I begin to realize my inactivity ... I could

Bore you to death.

I am inadequate, you can't reach me unless you

Touch me -

I can't help but feel that you don't.

Empty.

Your heart is spilled elsewhere

Dripping

Into the wind that sweeps tears from my face,

Stained

By your drops that burn into the flesh

Engraving

Into the mind what is too painful to process:

Possibility.

Unaware.

Two ships adrift at sea
Distressed, lonely.
Sending signals of help in vain.
Fog as thick as a man's hand
Making signals impossible to see
And difficult to steer
And they drift past each other
Inches apart, each sensing the presence of the other,
Yet unaware.

Communication possible – if only the fog would clear.
But now, like a man's hands clasped, the fog would swell
If only a pair of lips would tell
But the hopelessness inside each vessel locks the jaws

And they drift past each other
Moments apart, each envisioning traces of the other
But unable to chart.

And they drift past each other
Arm's length apart, each –
If only one would reach.
But utter frustration immobilizes the limb
And with a jaded outlook, hope flickers too dim.

And as fate would have it,
All of a sudden the fog would clear.
And just like the fog, the ships disappear
And the sea covers their tracks as if the ships were never there.
But they continue, now worlds apart
Looking for some remote sign of a way to survive,
Or even a new start.
But they drifted past each other.
Now on a fruitless search to nowhere.
The sea keeps that instance a secret

And they sail on...

Unaware.

The Land of Oddz

Affectionately known as Oddz, is the land of Oddity
Where one leaves the food but eats the crumbs
The inhabitants are called Oddzies.
They call each other 'sore-thumbs'
But you can't call them that! They'll throw a fit!
Just say, "Hello!" to the Oddzie, "Hello!" That's it.

The people there are friendly in an 'Oddz' sort of way.
Yesterday they said hi to you,
But ignore you totally today.
Please. Don't let this upset you and cause you great sorrow.
It's an every-other-kind-of thing.
They'll talk to you tomorrow.

The Land of Normz

Affectionately known as Normz, is the land of
Normality
Where one leaves the crumbs but eats the food
The inhabitants are called Normzies.
They call each other 'hum-drums'
But you can't call them that! They'll throw a fit!
Just say, "Hello!" to the Normzie, "Hello!" That's it.

The people there are friendly in a normal way.
Today they'll say hi to you,
In fact every day!
Please. Don't let this bore you and cause you great
sorrow.
It's an every-day-sort-of thing.
They'll talk to you tomorrow.

The Oddzies and the Normzies

It's odd how the Oddzies think the Normzies are
strange
Because they eat the food and leave the crumbs,
And the Normzies assume a disturbed stance
And have the audacity to complain about the ants.
And it's funny how the Normzies believe the
Oddzies are weird
To leave the food but eat the crumbs
And later on hear scornful cries
Because they don't have enough shoes
To shoo all the flies.

The Abandoned Consensus

It's sad that the Oddzies and the Normzies
Don't think they could live together.
If they just used their heads they could brave any
weather.
Since the Oddzies leave the food and eat the crumbs
And the Normzies eat the food and leave the crumbs
There's a simple remedy for these silly sore-thumbs
And those stubborn hum-drums.
Let the Normzies eat the food and the Oddzies eat
the crumbs.
Then there would be no disturbed stance
And no complaining about the ants.
There would certainly be no disturbed cries
And no need for shoes to shoo the flies.
Please. Don't let this story cause great sorrow for us.
In life let us use their abandoned consensus.

The Depth of Love.

I'd fallen in deep.
I could not measure the depth
Inside me, I searched
For the good inside me;
I found none.
I now stand face to face with my sinful nature.
I now realize I cannot do this on my own.
I now realize my hopelessness,
my weakness,
my emptiness.
I now realize my nothingness
I now realize I cannot save me from myself.
Would you believe I actually tried?

And I had fallen in deep -
The depth I cannot measure;
I sank deeper and deeper.
Then I realized I needed the Help outside of myself.

One last attempt in total despair.
I cry for help, the same muffled immensely
by the murky sea of what is now trivial.

When I awoke -
It took me a while -
But I realized I had fallen in deep!
The depth? Beyond Measure!
Looking to that Help outside myself,
I found love.
And I've fallen in deep!
The depth beyond measure.
I dive deeper and deeper.
I now have hope, strength.
The void is gone.
I now have something to hold on to -
Well, Someone.
I have a Savior. He now lives in me.
Would you believe for us He actually died?
Ah! The depth of Love! Beyond Measure!

Thinking and Praying

I'm thinking of someone whose smile makes mine
appear for no reason at all.
Someone willing to listen to what I have to say – it
could be great or small.
I'm thinking of someone whose arms are open wide
And holds me and squeezes till I'm warm inside
I'm thinking...
I'm thinking...
I'm thinking of you.

I'm praying for someone whose love I'd hate to lose.
I'm praying for someone whose path only he can
choose.
I'm praying for someone who God wants to use.
I'm praying...
I'm praying...
I'm praying for you.

Preparation

I feel like I'm preparing for a journey
The Destination? Far, far away.
Right now I want to up and leave
But for now, here I must stay.

The Place is warm and peaceful,
Not cold and dreadful like where I am.
It's gentle and kind and accepts you as you are
But not like here, trying to dictate who I am.

Inside the Shelter, my soul longs to be draped in this
Place
Here, it moans from pain and discomfort incessantly
It longs for a way of escape to this Place,
Peace it seeks relentlessly

Some faces here I no longer care to see
With no intention to offend

But your countenances so depress me
I can't wait for victory at this journey's end.

But then again I torture myself.
Things as they seem to me may not be –
Or maybe I'm handling this trial all wrong.
Maybe the problem isn't you – but me.
What seems to others as small stuff now,
I see a gigantic pot cooking up strife.
Well, whatever it is, it's in God's hands now.
I've made enough mess of my short, weary life.

And I will not go down without a fight.
I leave it to God when I pray every night.
Even if we wrestle 'til morning light
I refuse to go down without a fight -

I will not let go 'til You bless me.

Even then I'll tighten my grip
I will not let go though they stress me

Even though all this is preparation for the trip.

Enough Said

The night will run but the day pursues.
The former catching the latter is inevitable.
The dogs aren't spared;
Every one's got its day,
And everyone knows
That while the sun still shines,
It's the perfect time to make hay.

In my few short years
I've learnt one thing among many -
Running and looking behind
Doesn't help you any;
It only makes you unprepared
For what you are about to find.

The same thing from which you ran,
When you turn, may meet you nose to nose.
Now you're close enough to breathe the vibe

Now you've got to work on what's inside
Too late! Already met eye to eye...
Hard luck – it's the path you chose.

So, the day just caught up with the night...
And guess which dog's day is today?
And now that we've got sunshine...
What do you say?
It's here now: what was ahead,
Now that we've got sunshine...
Enough said.

Melody Uncaught

Melody uncaught,
Elusive and free.
Why do you hide yourself from me?
You sit on the wind, brushing tree after tree
Then swirl from the branch to the river
Flowing right past me.
Will I lose you to the tornado
Or the tsunami?
Melody uncaught,
Elusive and free.

Maturity

Waiting for the little girl inside me
To realize what she wants
Is not always what she needs.

Waiting for the little girl inside me
To realize that fairy tale endings
Exist in only what she reads.

Waiting for the little girl inside me
To stop the rant and rave
If only she would realize the time she would save...

If only she grew up.

Choices, Whims and Fancies

Trees and flowers,
Rivers and streams.
Wind and raindrops,
The sun and its beams.

Bread and honey,
Dinner before juice;
Uno o doce -
I don't want to choose.

Pictures and paintings,
Peas and rice;
Noodles and tuna,
My health a high price.

Nuggets and ketchup,
Life and love;

Straight and narrow,
Pigeon and dove.

Mind and friend,
Needle and pen;
Awkwardly comfortable -
Means to an end.

Politics and poetry,
Poetry and time;
Thoughts and rivalry -
Yours and mine.

Satisfaction and misery,
Happiness and crime;
Rags and cleanliness,
Neither brandy nor wine.

Mixture of matters,
Barley and thyme.
Salt and sour crème,

Lemon and lime.

Chances and mishaps,
Confusion and strife;
Serious or jokingly,
Husband and wife.

Sanity or insanity,
Pineapple or grapes;
Vexation and vanity.
Dad liked bare windows,
Mum liked drapes.

Oh! Look out now!

I can feel that crazy streak comin', like
Your nose is runnin', like
The highs I get
When you say the things you do -
And that's my song right there:
When the rhythm is you walkin',

And the lyrics are you talkin',
And your life is the symphony everybody's
watchin'...

And I want a front row seat;
I got a front row seat!
I'm so wired,
Like, I never get tired -
'cause I keep remembering the things you said,
positive vibes keep resounding in my head.
All I do is smile;
It's been a while.
Now I want to tell people wherever I go,
Let's sit and talk again;
I want to hear you make me smile again.
Positive conversation with my friend,
Solutions to this madness that never seems to end.
Then spread the cure like a virus far and wide
Heroes you and I are, inside,
'Cause the positivity we can no longer hide;
We could change the world!

I love that crazy streak –

Hooked on positivity!

This one Thing.

The one thing that requires my sweat, blood and
tears
Is digging down in the dirt to get out my fears.
Accepting there is healing after the tears,
As I am abandoned on shore;
Watching my ship go out to sea.

The one thing that requires my sweat, blood and
tears
Is letting you be -
And loving me.

Square Peg

You know you don't belong there.
But too afraid to face that fear,
Lying to yourself that you don't care.
Ideas that could improve your world,
But you won't share.
You convince yourself you should stay here
But you can't control the growth, dear.
Are you sure the seams are sincere?
What will you do when they begin to tear?
Is there any benefit in make-it-fit?
Show me where.

Assurance

Sunlight shimmers;
grass blades dressed
in dew.

Space of heaven
Reflects depth of ocean,
cast blue.

Reminds me that
I am loved
by You.

Enough!

Leaving the store with six pairs of shoes,
but only got two feet.
Fussin' about all those clothes
and only got one back.
Chasing so many a silly dream.
Sometimes, I jus' wanna hold my head and scream:
"Enough is enough!"

Keep thinking that I should think about
what they think of me -
Nothing but an erupting volcano
of irrationality.
But it all boils back down to you
chasing many a silly dream
My heart gets inside my head and it will scream:
"Enough is enough!"

There seem to be so many options;

I don't know what to do!
I sit and I settle my head; my heart asks:
Is any of them like you?
And guess what...they don't measure up -
Not even close.
No more chasing silly dreams!
My heart sings inside my head;
It's so serene.
Why was I so afraid to trust?
And we look into each other's eyes and we know:
Enough is enough.

Been a While

It's been a while -

Grown a lot since my last mile

Made a couple more friends

Life is good and I can't complain

Got some lives to touch

And some wounds to let heal,

A wall to break down

And a few hearts to steal

(But I mean that in a good way, you know)

The chances the choices,

They come and they go

Somehow regret doesn't run the way it's supposed to flow

So...

I'm just sayin', it's been a while

Run Wid It!

This one's free flow,
So – run wid it!
Things don' go
the way they supposed to, you know,
so - run wid it!
When the hunch
sums up a bunch,
it's more than you can munch -
isn't it?
Jus' run wid it
till the flow is dry
I won' lie -
You just might cry -
But run wid it ...
You don' know 'til you try

"Jus' roll wid it,"
Someone said,

"You'll come up wid gold in it,
Like all over, out and into it,"
But, I'm so out of it
It's like having no luck in the consulate
How do I conjure it?
I don' know these things.
It's the Consummate...
How dare I pen such?
The Word consumes me
For nothing I touch

Was ever...
...make my soul smile
...make my heart laugh
...make my day

You make my soul smile.
You make my heart laugh.
You make my day.

The Salvific Balm

Bring me a balm
that fills the open wounds
of my lacerated heart.
Fetch me a firm and sturdy bandage
so it doesn't fall apart.
Pour in the oil, the ointment and the wine,
To treat and keep it clean.
Now gag me, so that I can't scream!

There is a Balm
that heals the sin-sick soul,
A Hand that holds me together
when life takes its toll.
When I am purged, anointed,
made pure and clean
I can open my mouth and sing,
"Jesus, Your salvation!"
Such a beautiful thing!

Teach me that prayer -
that strong belief
that shuts a lion's mouth.
Teach me obedience: to go north to Nineveh,
and not Tarshish to the south.
Rain down Your precious Holy Spirit
Like the evening's refreshing dew.
My soul's only Hope, Jesus, is You!

There is a Balm
That heals the sin sick soul,
A Hand that holds me together
When life takes its toll.
When I am purged, anointed,
Made pure and clean
I can open my mouth and sing
Jesus, Your salvation,
Such a beautiful thing!

There's nothing I can do to make me
worthy of Your grace.

No merit; can't take credit
when I gain my heavenly place.
The voids, the holes, the frays, the shreds,
in my life's horrid tapestry -
Jesus fills those spaces for me!

Jesus the Balm,
Who heals the sin sick soul
He can hold you together
When life takes its toll
Let Him purge and anoint you
Make you pure and clean
Open your heart and sing
Lord, Your Salvation
What a beautiful thing.

Just beautiful. So beautiful.
Lord, Your salvation is
Just a beautiful thing!

Blueprint

Blueprint.
Imprint:
Footprint.

Power Source:
Ever Lasting.
Ever Living.
Ever Loving...

Designer:
Same as above.

Instinct: built in.
Intrinsic: merely survive.

Complex creature:
Propelled to prosper;

Energy to endure,
Ignorant to the word 'insecure';

Born to win;
Oblivious to giving in.

My life, with Your will I align
By Your Strength and grace that meet and combine;

Created to stand fast.
Surmount. Surpass.

This is your blueprint.
Imprint. Footprint.

About The Author

Kineta is a Barbadian writer with a Christian upbringing. In her spare time, she loves to blog and listen to podcasts.

Writing has cathartic properties for many people; it was no different for Kineta. The poems, at the time they were originally written, were a type of psychological first aid, hence the name "Cotton Wool".

The collection became a book after many years of hesitating to share her thoughts with the world.

However, she finally resolved that sharing these poems could be helpful or enjoyable to read, offering inspirational cotton wool to the souls of others who are hurting.

www.ingramcontent.com/pod-product-compliance
Lightning Source LLC
LaVergne TN
LVHW010507160826
845677LV00012B/2713

* 9 7 8 9 7 6 9 6 9 0 3 0 1 *